CAN YOUR

OUTFIT

CHANGE THE

WORLD?

a popactivism book

CAN YOUR
OUTFIT
CHANGE THE
WORLD?

Erinne Paisley

ORCA BOOK PUBLISHERS

Cataloguing in Publication information available from Library and Archives Canada

Issued in print and electronic formats.
ISBN 978-1-4598-1306-9 (softcover).—ISBN 978-1-4598-1307-6 (pdf).—
ISBN 978-1-4598-1308-3 (epub)

First published in the United States, 2017
Library of Congress Control Number: 2017949687

Summary: This work of nonfiction in the PopActivism series for teens looks
at how teens can make responsible and eco-friendly clothing choices.

*Orca Book Publishers is dedicated to preserving the environment and
has printed this book on Forest Stewardship Council® certified paper.*

Orca Book Publishers gratefully acknowledges the support for its publishing programs provided
by the following agencies: the Government of Canada through the Canada Book Fund
and the Canada Council for the Arts, and the Province of British Columbia through the
BC Arts Council and the Book Publishing Tax Credit.

Edited by Sarah N. Harvey
Design by Jenn Playford
Front cover and flap images by Ute Muller
Back cover images by Shari Keller/Mehera Shaw, Miguel Medina/Getty Images, Amy Hansen
Author photo by Jacklyn Atlas

ORCA BOOK PUBLISHERS
www.orcabook.com

Printed and bound in Canada.

To my brother,
Stuart Paisley

CONTENTS

ACTIVISM

The creation of social and/or
political change.

POPACTIVISM

Activism fused with
pop culture.

popactivism

see change, share change, be change

"Buy less, choose well, make it last."

—Fashion icon Vivienne Westwood

1

A DRESS MADE OF HOMEWORK

IN MAY 2015 I GRADUATED FROM HIGH SCHOOL in Victoria, British Columbia. First there was the cap-and-gown ceremony, and then there was the highly anticipated prom. I didn't find my prom dress at the local mall or at a vintage store or even online. Instead, I created the dress in my living room with only some scissors, tape, ribbon and old math homework. Yup, that's right. My old math homework!

I had to create a few drafts of the dress to make sure it would actually hold together. I assembled the final dress with the help of my best friend, Emily Faris. It took us one whole day to make, and even though it seemed to stay together okay, we kept extra tape in our purses during prom, just in case. On the dress I wrote in red ink, *I've received my education. Not every woman has that right. Malala.org.* Then I donated the money I would have spent on a "real" prom dress to the Malala organization and encouraged others to do the same. In *Can Your Smartphone Change the World?*, the first book in the PopActivism series, I tell the story of how the

STUART PAISLEY

"paper prom dress for women's rights" went viral.

Before the story went viral, many parents and people in my school asked questions about what the dress was made of. Why did I choose math homework and not English homework? How was the dress held together? Why didn't I just wear a normal prom dress?

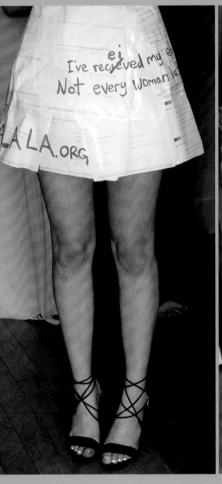

I carried extra tape in my purse to fix any rips that happened during the night! Here, my mom and Emily's mom repair a tear in my skirt. STUART PAISLEY

I've received my ei
Not every Woman has

ALA.ORG

THE MORE QUESTIONS I ANSWERED ABOUT MY PAPER DRESS AND THE REASON I WAS WEARING IT, THE MORE I THOUGHT ABOUT THE STORY BEHIND ALL MY CLOTHING.

The first sketch I ever drew of the paper dress.

SENDING A POSITIVE MESSAGE

The more questions I answered about my paper dress and the reason I was wearing it, the more I thought about the story behind all my clothing. The dress had started life as a tree, and then it became the paper I wrote on in a classroom. But where had my favorite pair of jeans come from originally? When I put on jeans and a graphic T-shirt the day after prom, I noticed how soft the material felt against my skin compared to paper, but I also wondered what the story of this outfit was. The T-shirt had a message on it too—it said *Less and Local*. What message and type of company was I supporting by wearing it? Did I agree with what that company stood for?

We all wear clothing of some sort every day. What you choose to wear becomes part of your identity, but it doesn't affect just you. Our clothing sends a message to the world around us, whether we want it to or not. But often we don't know what that message truly is. What we wear comes from some material—either natural or synthetic.

How that material was grown or manufactured, how it was processed and how far it was shipped all have an impact on the earth's environment. The treatment, working conditions and salaries of the people who make our clothing have an unmeasurable effect on these workers and their families. The items we wear often display logos, slogans, phrases and labels. Do you support what they say about the world or the company that makes the clothing? Your outfit has a lot more power than you might have realized!

A NEW (TO ME) PAIR OF BOOTS

Buying ethically doesn't mean never buying anything new again. What it's really about is making your shopping decisions in a more *globally conscious* way even when you buy something new. I remember when I first realized how important it is to understand the full history of the clothing most of us wear—where it comes from, who makes it, how it's made, how far it's traveled, its impact. I was supposed to buy a new pair of rain boots with my mom. We were in the store, and I started looking at where the rain boots were made. None of the labels told me anything about the conditions under which the boots were made or their environmental impact. There was no way to know whether any of these boots were ethically made, and I was very upset. I remember being overwhelmed by the thought of all the things I had bought in the past and all the things I would buy in the future that were not 100 percent ethically made. How was I ever going to shop for clothes again if I wanted to be kind to the earth and everyone who lives on it?

My mom and I talked about it for a long time. I soon realized that making the fashion world more ethical doesn't mean that every single thing we buy has to be bought in an ethically conscious way (although that would be amazing). Instead, it means that we can choose to make small decisions that lead to a better future. I didn't buy those rain boots. Instead, I bought secondhand rain boots from a store down the road. You might decide you don't really need that new pair of ripped jeans (instead

I recently found these red rain boots on sale in a secondhand store. They were a sustainable choice I could easily get behind!
JENN PLAYFORD

FASHION IS AN ART FORM, AN INDUSTRY AND AN INFLUENTIAL TOOL THAT CAN EMPOWER A COMMUNITY, MAKE PEOPLE FEEL ACCEPTED OR PROUD, AND EVEN HELP TO SAVE OUR PLANET'S ENVIRONMENT.

you could DIY them from secondhand jeans—see p. 87), or you could give away an old T-shirt instead of throwing it away. Congratulate yourself for any small step taken in a more ethical direction.

Fashion is an art form, an industry and an influential tool that can empower a community, make people feel accepted or proud, and even help to save our planet's environment. It's a tool you already have—and it's up to you to learn more about how you want to wield it. Your outfit definitely doesn't have to be made of paper to change the world. Every day when we wake up and choose what to wear, we have the opportunity to make a difference. Are you ready to join this #FashionRevolution or even start your own?

ARE YOU READY TO JOIN THIS #FASHIONREVOLUTION OR EVEN START YOUR OWN?

The Canadian company Preloved uses reclaimed vintage clothing, deadstock and overrun fabrics to create unique garments. **IAN MARTINS**

"The wider world perceives fashion as frivolity that should be done away with. The point is that fashion is the armor to survive the reality of everyday life. I don't think you can do away with it. It would be like doing away with civilization."

—*Bill Cunningham,*
American fashion photographer (1929-2016)

2

WHERE DO YOUR CLOTHES REALLY COME FROM?

ALL YOUR CLOTHING IS MADE FROM something that either grows in a field or is made in a lab. A lot of our clothing is made from cotton, one of the most heavily *irrigated* crops in the world. Growing it uses up a *lot* of precious water. In fact, it typically takes 2,720 liters (718 gallons) of water to create a single T-shirt, which is the amount of water most people drink over three years! Cotton is also the most heavily pesticide-sprayed crop in the world. *Pesticides* are chemicals that keep insects or diseases

off plants, which allows them to grow better. But they are also harmful to the environment and the health of people exposed to them.

Other natural fibers include linen, which is made from the fibers of the flax plant, and wool, created from the fleece of sheep and animals such as camels and alpaca.

Polyester is another material used to create a lot of clothing. Polyester is not grown in soil. It is made from petroleum, coal, air and water. So you might actually be wearing a form of gasoline right now! Polyester can be *recycled* and reused, but it is not *biodegradable*. When a piece of polyester clothing is thrown out, it does not break down and become part of our earth again the way natural fabrics can. This means polyester is harder on our environment than other more natural materials are.

POLYESTER CAN BE RECYCLED AND REUSED, BUT IT IS NOT BIODEGRADABLE.

Polyester was popular in the 1960s, so many vintage shops still stock clothing made from this material. Although it is not biodegradable, reusing it keeps it out of landfills and discourages the purchasing of new materials. JENN PLAYFORD

DON'T DUMP THAT DYE!

Many fabrics need to be dyed during their first stage of creation. Have you ever wondered how your jeans become the color they are? Jean fabric does not naturally come in a deep blue. Jeans have to be dipped in different types of chemicals to get this color. Unfortunately, these chemicals are usually not very environmentally friendly. If they are not disposed of properly, they can really hurt the environment. In China, some of the rivers have turned a toxic red because of all the chemical pollution from clothing factories. Talk about being able to see the environmental impact of some of our clothing choices!

The creation, transportation and discarding of clothing can have massive negative effects on our environment. All of these things contribute to *global warming*. Global warming is the term used by scientists to describe the rise in the temperature of the earth's atmosphere and oceans. Global warming leads to climate change. Global warming is caused by many human actions, including burning fossil

PP (potassium permanganate) spray, a harmful chemical used for pant washing, is seen running from these jeans in a Bangladesh RMG (ready-made garment) factory.
FAHAD FAISAL/WIKIPEDIA.ORG

3-D crunching, whiskers and wrinkles are added to jeans, to give denim a worn look and make them look more lived-in. FAHAD FAISAL/WIKIPEDIA.ORG

fuels (mostly gasoline), using pesticides, irrigating crops and filling up landfills with nonbiodegradable materials. You can learn more about climate change by following Greenpeace on social media or visiting its website www.greenpeace.org. Greenpeace is a global organization that helps to promote a greener and more peaceful world.

HEMP IS USUALLY GROWN PESTICIDE-FREE AND NEEDS MUCH LESS IRRIGATION THAN COTTON.

Luckily, environmentally friendly fabric alternatives are being developed every day. Hemp is usually grown pesticide-free and needs much less irrigation than cotton. It feels very similar to cotton when made into clothing and is even more breathable than cotton. There is also recycled polyester, which uses only pre-existing polyester to create new clothing. Bamboo is also a very environmentally friendly fabric since it is most often grown with very few (or no) chemicals and the plant itself is renewable.

POP QUIZ

Do you know what materials your clothing is made from?

Check the labels on your clothes to see what was used to make what you wear.

Google the impact of these materials and research some environmentally friendly alternatives if what you are wearing isn't good for our environment.

RANA PLAZA

Once all these fabrics have been created, they are shipped to factories where they are made into the clothing you buy.

Many clothing factories in developing countries have unsafe working conditions for their employees. In 2013, the Rana Plaza factory collapsed in Bangladesh while many workers were inside producing clothing for North American brands like H&M, Primark, the Gap, Mango and Walmart. The collapse killed 1,135 workers and severely injured another 2,515. People knew that the Rana Plaza garment factory was unsafe, but many employees had to keep working because of contracts they had been tricked into signing. Others had no other work options and had to feed their families, and some were threatened with violence if they left or asked for better working conditions. Their *human rights* were not protected.

Almost all of those killed were women and children. When children are forced to work under these inhumane conditions, it is called *child labor.*

Rana Plaza garment factory
after its collapse in 2013.
BAYAZID AKTER/DREAMSTIME.COM

Iqbal Masih and Free the Children

When Iqbal Masih was four, his family borrowed money from the owner of a carpet factory in Pakistan. To pay off this debt, Iqbal was sent to work in the factory for an indefinite amount of time. This is called **bonded child labor** or **debt slavery**.

He had to work under inhumane conditions and did not go to school. When he was ten years old, he escaped and joined the Bonded Labour Liberation Front. He was able to help over 3,000 other children escape similar situations. Iqbal was murdered when he was twelve, but his story has inspired others to continue to fight for better treatment of children all over the world.

The co-founders of Free the Children, Marc and Craig Kielburger, started their **nonprofit** when Craig heard Iqbal's story and was inspired by his fight for human rights. Free the Children is now an international nonprofit that also works with WE Day to empower children all over the world to help other children. You can get your school or community involved with Free the Children by going to we.org.

In 2014 I was selected as one of ten Canadians to travel to London, England, and attend the first ever WE Day UK. I got to see Malala speak live about activism! ERINNE PAISLEY

There are over 250 million children worldwide forced to work under conditions like these. Many of these children are employed by *sweatshops*. *The Otesha Book: From Junk to Funk* states that sweatshops are "any workplace where workers are subjected to extreme exploitation, including low wages (lower than the living wage), long hours, working conditions that endanger safety or health, and/or denial of basic human rights. A sweatshop can exist even when the factory is following local laws." In Bangladesh, garment workers make on average only a quarter of the legal living wage. This means that after long hours of working in horrible conditions, they will not earn enough money to have access to basic human needs like clean water, food and shelter.

SWEATSHOPS ARE "ANY WORKPLACE WHERE WORKERS ARE SUBJECTED TO EXTREME EXPLOITATION."

The fashion industry hasn't always had factories *offshore*. Clothing used to be made locally. In fact,

Inside a jeans-making factory in China, where material is sewn for Levi's.
LOGIT/DREAMSTIME.COM

A child working at a textile factory in Delhi, India.
PAUL PRESCOTT/DREAMSTIME.COM

Inside a Forever 21, an example of a fast-fashion chain.
TSORBIS/SHUTTERSTOCK.COM

only fifty-five years ago, 95 percent of all clothing sold in the United States was also made there. But when *fast fashion* really took off in the late 1990s, more and more clothing companies decided to use factories far away. This caused a big change in the *supply chain* for clothing, or how clothing is created from start to finish. Fast fashion encourages consumers to buy more (and cheaper) products so the clothing companies can increase their profits. There used to be only two main fashion seasons— summer/spring and autumn/winter. Today, new fashion seasons seem to occur almost every week, and most clothing sold in North America is made offshore, where it's easier to get away with violating employees' human rights. The more clothing created under these conditions, the cheaper and faster it can be sold. But the cost to human beings and to the environment is huge.

The fashion industry is one of the most environmentally destructive industries in the world— second only to the oil industry. It employs millions of people, often under inhumane conditions. And we are all a part of its cycle in one way or another.

These realizations about the clothing industry can be overwhelming—but there's hope! Being part of the constant clothing cycle—and let's face it, most of us are—can be a good thing too, because once you are aware of how it works, you have the power to change it. You have more *influence* than you might think. In fact, your outfit may even be able to change the world!

The FAIRTRADE logo helps you shop responsibly.
JENN PLAYFORD

Human Rights

Human rights are defined as rights that should be available to every single person on earth. The Universal Declaration of Human Rights, an official document explaining what these human rights are, was created by the United Nations in 1948. This was the first time "universal human rights" were put down on paper and declared to need protection. Some of these rights include the right to freedom of expression and the right to equal pay. Today, the declaration has been translated into over 500 different languages—you can read it yourself online on the UN website.

3

FASHION
DETECTIVE

I WAS ONCE TOLD "YOU VOTE WITH YOUR DOLLAR."
At the time, it wasn't quite clear to me what that
meant. When you buy new underwear, what
could you possibly be voting for? I soon came to
realize that when you spend money, you are also
supporting a company and its ethics (or lack of
ethics). If you buy from a company that treats its
workers inhumanely, then you are "voting" for that
kind of abuse to continue by giving the company
money and ensuring its success. Most people are

not going to be able to check the details of everything they buy in their life, but it's cool to think about the effect that buying one piece of ethically made clothing can have on our world. If you take the time to research and support companies that contribute positively to our world, then you are helping that company, its workers and the environment. With every dollar you spend, you are increasing the demand for that item and actually creating the funds for more of it. Every dollar you spend has power attached to it, which means you can make a difference every time you shop. So what do you want to see more of in the world?

EVERY DOLLAR YOU SPEND HAS POWER ATTACHED TO IT, WHICH MEANS YOU CAN MAKE A DIFFERENCE EVERY TIME YOU SHOP.

It is definitely not easy to consciously spend your money to support ethical companies. Clothing companies that use unethical means of production

POP QUIZ

Do you know what you are supporting when you spend money on clothes?

The Internet can help you become a fashion detective. You can research a brand you like by viewing the company's policies on the company website (often under *About Us*). You can also talk to people who work at your favorite stores. Ask if they know where the clothes are made and under what conditions. If they don't know, you can start a conversation that may make them curious about the company they work for.

don't go around advertising the fact. You have to dig deeper to figure out which clothing companies are working for the better good, and which are using harmful shortcuts to create cheaper products. Searching for this information, and the full story of your clothing, is a lot like being a fashion detective.

CHECK THAT LABEL!

Clothing labels can tell you a lot about the company you're choosing to support with your dollars. Sometimes the terms on labels can be confusing, but don't worry—they're easy to decode.

Fairtrade labels are put on clothing that have met a certain ethical standard. Fairtrade Canada registers companies with its third-party certification system after it has made sure the product is being produced in a way that has a positive social, economic and environmental impact. There is also a World Fair Trade Organization Standard that works in a similar way.

Organic is another positive label to look for. Clothing that has a registered organic symbol on it

Clockwise from top left: ME to WE's very own clothing brand; an eco-brand label; alchemy fashions uses the phrase *ethically made* on its tags; Hemp & Company labels list the materials used; Weave Creations includes *Earth Friendly* on its labels; Fair Trade Federation-approved label; Flying Heart labels identify *certified organic cottons.* JENN PLAYFORD

Do You Need a Bag for That?

Next time you are about to buy something (not just clothing), look at how much packaging it has. Is it really necessary? How much waste is the packaging producing? Choose products that have as little packaging as possible, and say no to plastic bags. You can also create a petition for free on Change.org, asking a company, organization or person to reduce unnecessary packaging. Get your friends and family to sign your Change.org petition, share your petition on social media, and remember to tag the organization to get its attention.

has been made from materials that were produced without the use of harmful chemical pesticides and herbicides.

Biodegradable fabric is environmentally friendly because it produces less pollution during production and decomposes quickly, without creating toxic aftereffects, fumes or runoffs, when thrown out.

If the label says *Recycled Materials,* it means the material used to make the clothing may have been a different item of clothing or even a disposable water bottle before becoming what you have in your hands.

#FASHREV

Sometimes the label can't tell you the full story of your clothing, and even when you do some detective work online or in person, it's still hard to figure out the history of your outfit. But don't worry—you don't have to be a fashion detective all on your own! There is power in numbers, and #fashrev (it stands for Fashion Revolution, a global movement that has an annual hashtag campaign encouraging people to tweet #whomademyclothes) uses this power to create even more change in the fashion world. Every year from April 18 to 24, people who are a part of #fashrev come together as fashion detectives online—and keep asking #whomademyclothes until they get satisfactory answers.

YOU HAVE TO GO DEEPER TO FIGURE OUT WHICH CLOTHING COMPANIES ARE WORKING FOR THE BETTER GOOD.

Fashion Revolution asks clothing companies for the true story of their products and brings attention to aspects of the fashion world we might not usually think about. People all around the world, including *you*, can join the fashion revolution by taking a selfie wearing your favorite piece of clothing, turned inside out so the label is showing. Then tweet your selfie that clothing brand using the hashtags #whomademyclothes and #fashrev. This asks the company to share the true story of where their clothing comes from.

POP QUIZ

What brand is your favorite T-shirt?

Does that brand talk about where and how its clothing is made?

Try to find out the full story of your clothing during the next Fashion Revolution Week by turning your clothing inside out and taking a selfie that asks #whomademyclothes.

Young activists pose during Fashion Revolution Week and ask, "Who made my clothes?"
BRYAN BERRY PHOTO

"Who made my clothes?"
—Fashion Revolution

Opposite page, top left: Emma from backofthewardrobe.com asks
Topshop who made her clothes. RACHEL MANNS
Opposite, left, and above: Mehera Shaw is a fair-trade garment manufacturer located
in Jaipur, India. The staff posed for these photos for Fashion Revolution Day.
SHARI KELLER/MEHERA SHAW

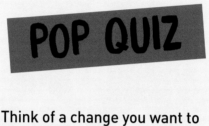

POP QUIZ

Think of a change you want to see in the fashion world. Can you write a *manifesto* that describes this change clearly? How many people can you get to sign it and show their support? You can put it online or mail it to your targeted fashion brand or organization once you've gotten enough signatures to have some impact.

Together, all of these #fashrev tweets have put pressure on the fashion world to create higher standards for how and where clothing is made.

Fashion Revolution has been going since 2013 and has more than 50,000 followers on its Instagram account, where the team posts year-round about where your clothes originate and the impact they have on the world around us. On past #fashrev days, I have tweeted selfies in my favorite H&M shirt to @hm.

DETOXING FASHION

In 2011, Greenpeace did some serious fashion detective work. After finding out more about the fashion industry's effect on the earth, they sent out a request to some of the world's biggest clothing brands: *stop releasing hazardous chemicals.* They called this movement #DetoxFashion. As we learned earlier, many harmful chemicals are often used to manufacture fabric, and they can irreversibly hurt our earth's environment. Greenpeace put a Detox Fashion Manifesto on its website that anyone can sign, asking big clothing companies to create a smaller, greener footprint on our planet. It reads:

1. We believe that brands and suppliers must act immediately to stop poisoning waterways around the world with hazardous chemicals.

2. We recognize that this will not happen overnight, and want brands and suppliers to be transparent about what chemicals they are releasing into the environment on the road toward toxic-free fashion. It is our water; we have a right to know.

3. We believe in rewarding and collaborating with honest and progressive suppliers and brands, and will encourage others to do the same.

Fashion brands want you to give them money. If enough people say they will only give their money to brands that operate ethically, they just might make some changes in the way they do business.

Over half a million activists, fashion designers and bloggers have paid attention to #DetoxFashion and committed to detoxing their clothing in the future. Even big brands like H&M, Nike, Adidas and Zara have promised to work toward having a greener footprint.

IF ENOUGH PEOPLE SAY THEY WILL ONLY GIVE THEIR MONEY TO BRANDS THAT OPERATE ETHICALLY, THEY JUST MIGHT MAKE SOME CHANGES IN THE WAY THEY DO BUSINESS.

Walking the Talk

A company's commitment to change is only a promise. In 2013, Greenpeace created the Detox Catwalk to check up on companies that had agreed to the #DetoxFashion manifesto and see if they were keeping their promises. Greenpeace created a YouTube video to show the world how much (or how little) companies had done to keep their promise of detoxed fashion. You can follow the progress of #DetoxFashion through the Detox Timeline at greenpeace.org or on YouTube.

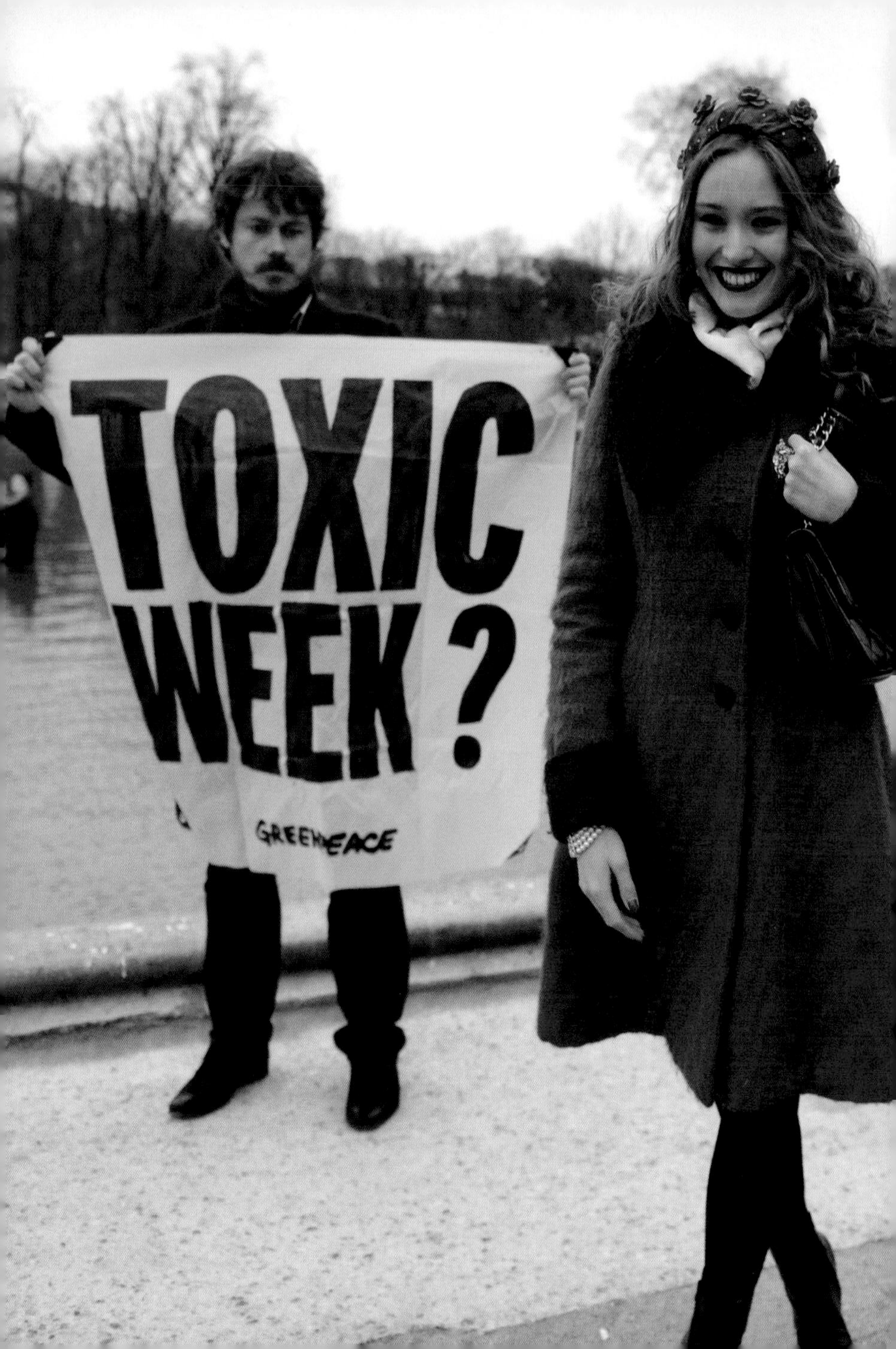
TOXIC
WEEK?

During Paris Fashion Week 2013, Greenpeace members mounted their Detox Fashion campaign. Protesters held up their signs in Tuileries Garden while a fashion-week attendee posed in front of them.
MIGUEL MEDINA/GETTY IMAGES

"We carry the story of the people who make our clothes around with us."

—*Ali Hewson*

4

POSITIVE BRANDS

THERE ARE GREAT BRANDS OUT THERE to invest your money in, but sometimes they can be hard to find. Fortunately there are websites and blogs whose sole purpose is to make this search easier for you. Here are some of my favorites:

1) *Freestate* (shopfreestate.com) is a blog that has an online brand directory that lets you search for whatever you may need and comes up with ethical companies that sell it.

2) *Style Wise* (stylewise-blog.com) was created to discover and talk about fair trade and sustainable fashion online. The blog focuses on being stylish *and* ethical.

3) *Eco Fashion World* (ecofashionworld.com) is not only a blog but also a search engine for ethical fashion brands. You can search by brand, store, category, eco criteria or country.

4) *The Good Trade* (thegoodtrade.com) is an online community that allows readers to discover and share new brands, products and ideas that are contributing positively to our world.

POSITIVE FASHION BRANDS

Finding new ethical brands can be very exciting! But they can be hard to find, even for fashion detectives. To start you off on your own hunt for earth-friendly fashion, here are some of my favorite brands.

PATAGONIA

Patagonia is famous for its outdoor wear. Its supply chains are "fair, safe, legal and humane," and it gives

Patagonia stores sell clothing produced through ethical supply chains. JENN PLAYFORD

ON BLACK FRIDAY IN 2016, PATAGONIA PLEDGED TO GIVE 100 PERCENT OF ITS GLOBAL AND RETAIL SALES TO GRASSROOTS NGOS WORKING TO HELP THE ENVIRONMENT.

1 percent of all sales to worldwide environmental organizations. On Black Friday in 2016, Patagonia pledged to give 100 percent of its global and retail sales to organizations that were working to help the environment. Usually Black Friday sales encourage consumers to spend money on new clothing (and other items), which adds to our environmental footprints in a negative way. Instead, Patagonia raised over $10 million to help our planet! Patagonia is also unique in the fashion world because it encourages consumers to wear Patagonia clothing until it wears out instead of constantly replacing it with new items (the way fast fashion encourages us to do). Its Worn Wear program celebrates stories of people wearing Patagonia clothing through many years.

POP QUIZ

Do you want to share your fashion detective skills with the world?

Start your own blog for free at wordpress.com, weebly.com or tumblr.com. You can choose from a number of themes and share your blog on social media for others to discover. On my blog, PopActivism.com, there is a section called "Conscious Clothing" where I talk about how I have investigated some of my favorite brands to see how ethical they really are.

Some people have bodysurfed in their board shorts for four years, and others have worn their fleece through six seasons of tree planting. There's even a *Worn Wear* movie on YouTube with half a million views! You can submit your own story about wearing Patagonia for as long as possible to worn-wear.patagonia.com. You might even be featured on their website.

TOMS

TOMS is the original creator of the "one for one" ethical clothing model. The company was a viral success when it created the concept that for every shoe you buy, another pair is given to someone in need. It also provides a full medical eye exam to someone who couldn't otherwise afford it when you purchase sunglasses, and gives out safe birthing materials to a community in need when you buy a bag. It even provides bullying prevention and response programs when you buy a High Road backpack. Talk about fashion that gives back!

TOMS shoes created the model of "one for one" clothing sales, which many other companies have now adopted. These TOMS were designed for a wedding! JOSHUA RAINEY PHOTOGRAPHY/SHUTTERSTOCK.COM

TENTREE

Tentree does exactly what its name says—for every clothing purchase, it plants ten trees. Simple as that. The Canadian company was started by two college students, Dave Luba and Kalen Emsley, in 2012. Since then they have planted over 8.5 million trees all over the world, all funded by company sales. When you buy something, you get a tree code so you can track online exactly where your ten trees were planted. There are over 12 million trees being cut down each day (yes, that's *million*), many without any new trees planted in their place. In fact, it is calculated that every *second*, one and a half acres of rainforest is cut down. This has a seriously negative effect on the environment. You can follow tentree on social media to see more of its tree-planting projects. The company's Instagram account alone has over 1.5 million followers.

Tentree is based on an environmentally friendly idea that two friends came up with. Now it is a massive company creating change every day.
ZHUKOVSKY/DREAMSTIME.COM/JENN PLAYFORD

61

THE STORY BEHIND THINGS

Stories Behind Things is an Instagram blog about creating a sustainable and conscious culture. Founders Jemma and Ella believe that the culture around clothing and style can be shifted through storytelling. Each Instagram post features the story of where their clothing came from. Their pieces are usually vintage, locally made or ethically sourced. Jemma and Ella encourage their followers to slow down and make choices about the brands they support and what types of products they consume. Through storytelling they are shifting the culture around fast fashion, and their community of conscious consumers has already grown to over 12,000!

Jemma and Ella each have a social media following, which they often use to promote ethical consumerism and their blog.
JEMMA AND ELLA/ STORIES BEHIND THINGS

You can follow Jemma and Ella's ethical fashion adventures on Instagram @storiesbehindthings.
TOBY HART

PEOPLE TREE

People Tree aims to have all parts of its supply chain certified fair trade—from the farmer to the artisan. This means fair prices are paid to all workers involved in creating its clothing, no matter where they are working or at what stage of production. The company does this in many different ways, including using sustainable resources, such as organic, pesticide-free cotton, and making sure all of its clothing is dyed using safe, chemical-free dyes.

KHOGY

Did you know that fish is one of the most popular foods in the world? Unfortunately, processing fish produces massive amounts of waste. Jenny and Caroline Al decided to turn discarded fish skins into a type of leather for clothing, shoes and bags. To create this stylish new material, they naturally dye the fish skins. Most leather requires the killing of many cows, but this type of leather uses only animal products that have already been thrown out. There's definitely nothing fishy about this idea. If you visit www.khogy.com you can watch their two-minute video explaining how fish-skin leather can create fantastic new fashion!

KROCHET KIDS INTL.

Krochet Kids wants to empower everyone who is part of the company—starting with those who make the clothing. Creators in Uganda and Peru are given fair wages as well as the chance to take part in education and mentoring programs. The company itself is nonprofit, which means its main purpose is not to make a *profit* but to invest back into its own initiatives. Not only that, but every single product is signed by the person who made it. Talk about knowing who made your clothes! You can even thank the creator of your clothing on the Krochet Kids website (www.krochetkids.org) by writing a letter directly to them. On the company's YouTube channel there is a video of some creators receiving these letters. When a simple thank-you can mean so much, why waste the chance to say it?

> THE COMPANY ITSELF IS NONPROFIT, WHICH MEANS ITS MAIN PURPOSE IS NOT TO MAKE A PROFIT BUT TO INVEST BACK INTO ITS OWN INITIATIVES.

URBAN RENEWAL

URBN is a group of global consumer brands comprised of Urban Outfitters, Anthropologie, Free People, BHLDN, Terrain and the Vetri Family. The Urban Outfitters brand has over 200 locations worldwide. Its regular clothing lines are not necessarily ethically made, but its Urban Renewal collections definitely are. UO releases a number of different collections of clothing each year, and the Urban Renewal line consists strictly of updated and reimagined vintage pieces. These recycled fashion items are fairly affordable and 100 percent stylish.

Urban Renewal's all-gender sign on fitting rooms in London, England. JENN PLAYFORD

In fact, almost all of UO's summer 2016 jean shorts were made from previously worn jeans. The only catch with reimagined vintage items is that when they sell out, more cannot be mass produced, so you better get them while they're hot! It would be great if everything UO made was as ethically responsible as the Urban Renewal line—but it's a great start.

URBAN RENEWAL
REMADE VINTAGE RECYCLED

Urban Renewal carries many different styles of clothes, all ethically made! JENN PLAYFORD

POP QUIZ

What type of products do you want to see in your favorite stores?

Email your favorite store and tell the staff what type of products you'd like them to sell. You can find a store's email on its website, or you can message the staff directly through any of their social media accounts. Let them know what you'd like to spend your money on and why. You can also tweet praise at companies and specific brands that produce ethical collections. Continue to question the way things are and, more important, the way things can be!

THINX

THINX is a company that has created underwear designed to absorb menstrual flow. On its website it says *THINX are made to be a backup to tampons or menstrual cups, though some opt to use it as a replacement on lighter days.* Did you know that over 100 million girls in the developing world fall behind in school just because of their periods? Girls do not have access to anything that can catch their menstrual flow, so they miss up to two weeks of school a month because they have no option other than bleeding in public. If they fall too far behind to catch up, eventually they will be forced to drop out. From the very beginning, THINX has been committed to helping those girls stay in school. For every purchase, the company also gives some of the funds to AFRIpads, a company in Uganda that produces sustainable menstrual pads. These pads can keep more girls in school worldwide. THINX wants to change the taboo and shame around menstruation. They urge girls and women to "bleed for female empowerment"!

SMOKING LILY

All of Smoking Lily's designs are conceived and created in their Victoria, British Columbia, studio. It's located in a secret loft space, which I was lucky enough to be able to visit in 2017.

The moment I stepped into the space, it was clear how much passion goes into every single piece of clothing. Employees were hard at work doing everything from sewing the fabrics to creating new designs. The owner says that Smoking Lily has worked hard to become a zero-waste company. Clothing is produced with a variety of materials, from bamboo to vintage fabrics to dead stock (left-over fabric from larger companies that would otherwise be thrown out). At Smoking Lily it's never a question of who created your clothes—you can check out their Instagram or Facebook page to meet virtually almost every employee who works there and even read editorials from the founder, Trish Tacoma.

At Smoking Lily it's easy to find out who created your clothes.
JENN PLAYFORD

SMOKING LILY HAS A NO-WASTE
POLICY, EVERY SCRAP GETS USED UP.

SMOKING LILY

POST NO BILLS

PRAY FOR PILLS

EVERY ITEM IS LOCALLY MADE, FROM SCREEN PRINT TO CONSTRUCTION.

The loft space where the Smoking Lily studio is located and each item is locally made.
JENN PLAYFORD

ETHICAL STORES

Sometimes you don't even have to do that much fashion-detective work to find a selection of ethical brands. A number of stores worldwide carry only positive fashion brands, and you can shop at a lot of them without leaving your bed. That's right, I'm talking about online clothing stores that only stock ethical and environmentally friendly products.

On Ecohabitude.com, you can search for your next wardrobe essential by ethical brand or by product footprint. Looking for a nontoxic yoga hoodie? They've got it. What about a sweatshop-free organic sweater? No need to look further! This online store seems to have an endless supply of ethical options, and you can even search the store from least expensive upward.

At Enrou.com, you can not only choose from a number of different ethical fashion brands but also track your direct impact. On Enrou's map you can find exactly where your purchase originated and look at the biography of the artisan who created it. You can even share the full story of your clothing on

In 2013, an exhibition called *So Critical So Fashion* displayed biodegradable, vegan and recycled materials during Milan Fashion Week.
EUGENIO MARONGIU/SHUTTERSTOCK.COM

Browsing sale items
at Not Just Pretty.
JENN PLAYFORD

social media by clicking the Share button. Enrou's brands also support other development projects in their artisans' communities, such as health education and financial coaching.

If you ever find yourself in Vancouver, British Columbia, you can browse in person through a number of ethical and eco-friendly fashion brands at Body Politic. In store they carry a number of sustainable designs, and staff are ready to answer any of your fashion-detective questions. In my hometown of Victoria, British Columbia, Not Just Pretty boutique sells only ethical fashion brands. And a

A PORTION OF NOT JUST PRETTY'S PROFITS GO TOWARD ONE OF ITS THREE FAVORITE CHARITIES.

portion of Not Just Pretty's profits go toward one of its three favorite charities: SeaChange Marine Conservation Society, Raincoast Conservation Foundation and Shaw Centre for the Salish Sea. Try to see if there are any ethical clothing stores in your area by Googling that phrase.

"Wear clothes that matter."

—*Solitaire Townsend*

5

REDUCE, REUSE AND RECYCLE

BEING A GLOBALLY CONSCIOUS FASHION CONSUMER doesn't have to mean just searching out and buying new ethical brands. From *charity* stores to auctions to clothing-swap parties, there are many other ways you can use fashion to change the world. Most follow the three Rs of being environmentally aware: reduce, reuse and recycle. By using the three Rs, you can gain new outfits without contributing to the production of any new clothes, which massively reduces your environmental and ethical footprint.

STORES THAT FOLLOW THE THREE Rs

Thrift, vintage and consignment stores can help you reduce, reuse and recycle clothing fashionably and sustainably. Instead of letting the clothes you no longer wear sit at the back of your closet unworn (or even worse, end up in a landfill), consider taking them to one of the following types of stores. You can also discover new-to-you fashion items here that no one else will have! Another phrase for reused clothing is *well loved*, because the clothing has been loved by a previous owner.

ANOTHER PHRASE FOR REUSED CLOTHING IS WELL LOVED.

So where is the best place to donate your old clothes and find great deals to replace them?

RESALE STORES

Resale stores take your clothing donations and give you store credit or cash in return for them. The store then resells them for a new price to the public. Sometimes resale stores are very picky about what they will buy from you because their store has a theme or type of clothing they are looking for, such as designer clothes or clothing from one specific period of history.

CONSIGNMENT STORES

Most consignment stores function in a similar way to resale stores because both of them are *for-profit*. Consignment stores agree to sell your clothing for you, and you only get paid for the clothing when it sells. The store takes a percentage (ask what it is before you leave your clothes) of the money your clothing sells for. If your items don't sell, they are returned to you, or you can opt to have them donated to a charity.

THRIFT STORES

Also called charity shops, thrift stores focus on giving their profits to a specific charity or not-for-profit organization. You can donate your used clothing to them so that they can resell it and raise more money for their charity. You can also buy new-to-you clothes for yourself. You've got to dig for the gold, but it's totally worth it and for a good cause! For instance, the Salvation Army has thrift stores across North America but is also a charitable organization. Its money goes toward supporting vulnerable people in communities in over 120 countries around the world. It provides support in the form of homeless shelters, food, warm clothing and mental-health resources, among other things.

Value Village is a popular resale store, but you should be aware that it is owned by Walmart. That doesn't mean you should never shop there again; it's just good to know where your money is going so you can make informed choices. JENN PLAYFORD

Salvation Army volunteers work hard in their communities.

Many stores have both new clothes and sections dedicated to vintage clothing. JENN PLAYFORD

VINTAGE STORES

Vintage stores can be run like any of the stores listed above, but they only sell clothing from a specific time in history, like the 1940s or 1960s. You won't find anything that's been made in the last decade or so, but you can definitely find unique pieces because most of the vintage styles aren't even being created anymore. Talk about one of a kind!

Just like Macklemore & Ryan Lewis rap in their song "Thrift Store," you can pop some tags, discover the newest trend and help the world around us by shopping at stores that recycle clothing. No new resources will have been used to create the clothing you buy, and you'll prevent another piece of clothing from ending up in the landfill.

POP SOME TAGS, DISCOVER THE NEWEST TREND AND HELP THE WORLD AROUND US BY SHOPPING AT STORES THAT RECYCLE CLOTHING.

POP QUIZ

How many pieces of clothing can you clear out of your wardrobe right now?

Ask yourself whether you have worn a piece of clothing in the last year. If you haven't, then it might be time to let it go. Once you've gathered some clothes, head down to your local thrift or consignment store and let someone else enjoy your discarded clothes. While you're there, you can always check out what else the reuse stores have to offer.

SHOPPING THE THREE Rs ONLINE

There are a number of websites that make buying and selling used clothing super easy. On craigslist.com, for example, you can buy and sell almost anything online. There are craigslist communities all over the world. Most people meet up in person to sell and buy from craigslist; stay safe by meeting in a public place and bringing another person with you.

On Etsy.com, you're encouraged to not only resell your used items but also sell handmade products, clothes and crafts. Etsy is like an online market where you can search for used items or unique things produced by people from all over the world. You can post your own creations or search for other people's. You can even message the creators personally before purchasing your newest handmade fashion staple.

CREATING YOUR OWN REPURPOSED CLOTHING

There are also ways to create a new wardrobe without buying a single new or used piece of clothing.

If you search for DIY *clothing* online, you can find creative ways to give new life to your current clothes. On Pinterest and similar sites there are directions on how to do everything from turning a pair of old "mom jeans" into cute new summer shorts to making cozy slippers from an old sweater. Once you've got a few projects under your belt, you could even create your own designs and share them with others online.

YouTube is a great place to search for DIY directions, because you can follow along with the video as you try to create a new look. One of my favorite YouTube DIY channels is TheSorryGirls,

YOUTUBE IS A GREAT PLACE TO SEARCH FOR DIY DIRECTIONS, BECAUSE YOU CAN FOLLOW ALONG WITH THE VIDEO AS YOU TRY TO CREATE A NEW LOOK.

based in Toronto, Ontario. They now have nearly one million subscribers and can show you how to turn an old blouse into a fashionable off-the-shoulder shirt or make a mini backpack from a thrift-shop purse.

POP QUIZ

What can you create or repurpose to sell online?

On eBay.com, you can buy both new and used products directly from sellers all over the world. NastyGal.com, an online clothing company that also sells vintage, got its start by reselling clothing on eBay. Now NastyGal.com is a major fashion outlet. Not only can you search for new socially conscious clothing deals online, but you could also set up an eBay.com account and sell your own creations online.

I'm wearing my DIY jeans created by distressing/ripping the legs and rolling/sewing the cuffs. JENN PLAYFORD

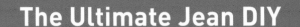

The Ultimate Jean DIY

My favorite pair of jeans is actually an old pair I "borrowed" from my mom (she didn't mind) and DIY'd. People still ask me where I bought them, and the look on their faces when I say they were free is wonderful every time—and even more wonderful when I can share some tips on how to make your own DIY creations! Try this DIY jeans project yourself by finding an old pair of jeans, drawing where you want holes to be on the legs, and cutting these holes with scissors. Then rub sandpaper along the holes to spread the material apart and give it a more "distressed" look.

POP QUIZ

What would you like to make from your used clothing?

Search for DIYs to reinvigorate your wardrobe without buying any new pieces. Make sure to take before and after pictures of your creation to share with others using the hashtag #DIY. Also include your tips and tricks with your pictures to make it easier for others to follow along.

There are also many online blogs that feature DIY's to fit any fashion season. UpcycleThat.com is another popular website for reusing things in innovative ways. You will find creative projects on UpcycleThat.com that aren't just for clothing. You can search the "Inspiration" section or *Make That, Use That* or *Buy That* on the drop-down menu bar, submit your own projects or view other upcyclers' projects.

CLOTHING SWAPS

Clothing swaps can be a really fun way to add to an ethical wardrobe. They allow you to reduce, reuse and recycle fashion with new and old friends. You can arrange to get together with a group of friends to exchange clothing that you haven't worn in a while. Other friends' "old styles" could turn into your new regulars. And it doesn't have to cost a thing!

If you're feeling ambitious, organize a clothing swap for your larger community—maybe at your school! You can publicize the event on Facebook and ask to use your school's gym. Or you can advertise more widely and hold the swap at a larger space that is open to the public, such as a community center.

Ethical Writers
Coalition Clothing Swap

The Ethical Writers Coalition in New York has thrown a number of large clothing-swap events in NYC, which have been great successes. New friends have been made, styles discovered, and ethical fashion designers have come out to premiere their new collections. All extra clothing was donated to the Clean Clothes Campaign.

The Clean Clothes Campaign is an organization that works worldwide to improve the working conditions, and protect the human rights, of those working in the clothing industry. You can learn more about these events, and similar ones, at EthicalWriters.co.

Work with other like-minded people to throw a clothing-swap party that brings attention to the issues around ethical shopping. You can even host guest speakers or representatives of ethical brands. You could also ask for donations from participants in the clothing swap to go toward a charity of your choice, and donate any leftover clothes to a local thrift store. These types of events can be a great opportunity to meet and learn from other people who are looking to stay fashionable while changing our world. The more people involved, the more clothing options you have to choose from.

There are many places online to list and search for the perfect clothing swap. In high school, I was part of a Facebook group called "Victoria Girls Swap and Shop," created for people to exchange their

THESE TYPES OF EVENTS CAN BE A GREAT OPPORTUNITY TO MEET AND LEARN FROM OTHER PEOPLE WHO ARE LOOKING TO STAY FASHIONABLE WHILE CHANGING OUR WORLD.

clothing with one another in my hometown of Victoria, British Columbia. The group grew to have over 3,000 members. You could search through items for sale, offer to swap items or sell your own clothing for money. I was able to sell a few of my own things to other people in my community and got some bargains on new-to-me clothes. If your city doesn't have one, you can always start your own Facebook group—you never know how large it might grow. Just be sure you stay safe when you exchange clothes with a stranger by meeting in a public place and bringing someone with you.

With the app and website Poshmark, you can list items in your closet for sale and search for others. There are Posh Party events, which happen online with the app, where you can buy and sell your items within a certain group of users. These groups could be made up of your own friends or strangers. On the app and website Yerdle Recommerce, no actual money is exchanged at all. Instead, when you list something on Yerdle.com and give it away, you earn Yerdle points. You can then use these Yerdle points get someone else's item.

POP QUIZ

Now that you've learned more about the power of clothing swaps, are you ready to host your first one?

Start small by inviting your close friends, in person or through a Facebook event, and create your own successful event. Maybe one day you'll be hosting a major public clothing-swap event!

"Be yourself, everyone
else is already taken."

—Oscar Wilde

6

DECODING FASHION MESSAGES

WHEN YOU TURN ON THE TELEVISION, watch a movie, pick up a magazine or go online, you are constantly being exposed to suggestions of what you should be wearing. Scroll through Facebook, tap through Twitter or tune in to YouTube, and the same thing happens. Whether it's specific brands telling you their clothes will make you "cooler" or new "haul" videos encouraging you to spend more and more, messages all around us tell us how we should act, what we should look like and what we should buy. How do we decode these messages? Why do they exist? Do we have to listen to them? Noticing the messages is definitely the first step in understanding them better and even changing them!

WHY DO WE WANT TO SPEND, SPEND, SPEND?

Did you know that in the United States alone over 12 million tons of clothing ends up in landfills each year? And only half of the population recycles its used clothing. Not only that, but according to *The True Cost*, a documentary on the negative effects of the fashion industry, more than eighty billion new pieces of clothing are consumed worldwide each year. This means a *lot* of people are buying a *lot* of new clothes and throwing old clothes into the trash nearly as fast. This process greatly damages the environment. With so many ways to reduce, recycle and reuse clothes, why do we keep buying (and throwing out) so much clothing?

A 2007 study by the market-research firm Yankelovich, Inc., estimated that any person living

Apps That Help You Buy Less

There are a number of apps that can help you start to change your consumer habits. The app Instead helps you put your money toward charitable endeavors instead of clothing. Instead wants you to ask, Do I really need this? The idea is that the next time you reach into your bag to pay for something, you first consider whether you really need that particular thing. Maybe you do, and that's okay. But maybe instead of buying more stuff, you can put your money toward causes like helping to provide clean water for others through the building of wells.

POP QUIZ

Do the models in your favorite magazines represent the community around you?

If not, write to the magazines and ask them to feature more diversity. Or even start your own magazine to celebrate the differences in each and every one of us!

in a large city is exposed to over 5,000 ads per day in various forms—on TV, radio, the Internet and even the sides of buses, or in newspapers and magazines. Most advertisements encourage us to buy more things because this will make more money for the companies that are selling them. Multiple fashion seasons are meant to make us buy more in order to keep up with new trends. But do we really need all of these *things*?

WHAT IS BEAUTIFUL?

Advertising doesn't just tell us to spend more. It also tries to tell us what is beautiful, handsome or cool, or what people should do based on their gender or race. In reality, all of these things can only be decided by you. You are the only person in the world who knows who you want to be, what you think is cool and what you believe is beautiful. So when advertising tells us there is only one version of these things, it can be hurtful and even encourage people to not be who they truly are.

DIVERSITY

Think about the type of person you usually see in advertisements for clothing—white, tall and thin. We are told that these images reflect what's "normal," when in fact they do not actually reflect the world around us. The fashion industry is still very far from representing all people equally. In fact, Fusion Media reported that in 2014 only 14 percent of American cover models were women of color. In 2017, during New York City Fashion Week, one of the four biggest fashion weeks in the world, almost 70 percent of the models were white. Not accurately representing diversity encourages discrimination. It tells the world to accept only one type of person as "normal" or "beautiful" or "cool" instead of showing

WE ARE TOLD THAT THESE IMAGES REFLECT WHAT'S "NORMAL," WHEN IN FACT THEY DO NOT ACTUALLY REFLECT THE WORLD AROUND US.

POP QUIZ

How can you help create more media and advertising that shows diversity?

Support, share and encourage positive ad campaigns and media messaging. *Boycott* companies that are running campaigns with inaccurate or negative messages. Write to them and let them know what you are doing. Watch and share positive media content. You can even create more diverse content of your own and share it through social media.

Ballet Shoes for Everybody

For as long as almost everyone can remember, "flesh-colored" dance shoes came in one shade: pale pink. This is not a "flesh" shade for every skin tone—there is much more diversity than that in our world. In response to this issue, dancewear brand Bloch worked with the Royal Ballet in the United Kingdom to make a line of ballet shoes that features different shades of "nude." Eric Underwood, an African American dancer, posted a video on Instagram showing how much time he has to spend pancaking makeup onto his "flesh-colored" ballet shoes to make them match his skin tone before each performance. After his video came out, the idea for this new line of ballet shoes began to take shape. The inclusive brand has now been written about on websites and news outlets such as BBC News.

the reality of a diverse population. Preventing equal work opportunities in the fashion world based on ethnicity is an act of racism.

Bethann Hardison is a former model who now works as an activist. In 2013 she co-founded the Diversity Coalition, which targets racial diversity (or the lack of it) in the fashion industry. In 2015 she wrote a blog entry about diversity in fashion for the *Business of Fashion* website that got shared nearly a thousand times.

There have been a number of magazines and initiatives created to fight the under-representation of minorities in the fashion industry. For example, *Native Max Magazine* is the first *ever* Native American fashion magazine. The mission of the company that produces it is to "educate and present the unique beauty of indigenous cultures. We are working to replace cultural appropriation with cultural appreciation by ultimately reshaping the indigenous media landscape." Native Max is a digital media company that produces videos and events; it even has its own Lifestyle app that you can download on your smartphone today.

Native Max's founder, Kelly Holmes, told ManRepeller.com in an interview, "As a teenager, I was going through magazines and I felt like I couldn't connect. I wished that there was something that could connect with someone like me. What if there was a Native magazine with Native American models wearing Native American designs and photos taken by Native American photographers? I went into my mom's room and told her about this idea and said, 'Someone should do this.' She said, 'Why don't you?' I went back into my room and I wrote down all of these ideas."

PHOTOSHOPPING

Before the mid-twentieth century, the standard of female beauty was largely "untouched" and natural, curves and all. For instance, Marilyn Monroe's curvaceous body type was seen as the ideal in the late 1950s and early 1960s, but now she would not be treated kindly by media. Society's idealized female body has become thinner and thinner over the years—and unrealistically flawless. In fact, many of the images you see of the "ideal woman" are not even real. Almost all advertising images are now Photoshopped to present an unrealistic beauty standard. Models and celebrities are Photoshopped to look skinnier or have larger lips and clearer skin. Makeup can require hours of work just to look "natural." Even mannequins are manufactured to represent an unrealistic weight and body shape.

ALMOST ALL ADVERTISING IMAGES ARE NOW PHOTOSHOPPED TO PRESENT AN UNREALISTIC BEAUTY STANDARD.

These unrealistic standards of "beauty" are usually impossible to achieve in real life in a healthy way. This can lead people to feel pressured to do unhealthy things—like starve themselves or undergo plastic surgery—in order to achieve these unrealistic ideals. In magazines, celebrities are shamed for "body flaws," reinforcing shame for ordinary people with real bodies. Advertisements sell their products as "cures" for beauty "flaws" we are all assumed to have.

A model is shown before and after professional makeup, hair and photoshopping. MAKSIM DENISENKO/SHUTTERSTOCK.COM

It's clear that there is a lot of pressure in our society to look a certain way. But many celebrities and some fashion brands are fighting against this and celebrating the natural differences and beauty in each and every one of us. For instance, in 2014 Zendaya posted a photo on Instagram of her magazine cover for *Modeliste* after she was shocked by how they had Photoshopped her body. One half of the picture showed the Photoshopped image and the other showed the original photo. She told her followers, *[I] was shocked when I found my 19 year old hips and torso quite manipulated. These are the things that make women self conscious, that create the unrealistic ideals of beauty that we have.* Zendaya then got the magazine to release the real picture and take down the Photoshopped images. Other celebrities who have protested Photoshopping include Lorde, Ashley Benson and Keira Knightley.

In spring 2014, Aerie released its Aerie Real campaign, which featured only unairbrushed models. #aerieREAL highlighted the fact that the photos were not retouched, and encouraged us all to embrace what we love about our own bodies.

GENDER ROLES

Advertising not only tells us what we should look like or what is "normal"; it often tells us how we should behave too. Modern advertisements often sell clothes by portraying women in hypersexualized roles. This *objectifies* women, which means women are seen only as sexual objects instead of being seen as people with diverse qualities and abilities. This limits the world's view of what women can be—which is anything they want to be!

As well, many advertisements portray "being a real man" as being hypermasculine—someone who doesn't show emotions, is physically strong and usually wears darker colors, among other things. In reality, "being a man" can only be defined by that man himself. There are no real limits on what a man can be or what he should wear.

Most clothing brands sort clothing styles by gender, but this limits the many expressions of gender that exist in our world. Since clothing is a means of self-expression, there is no reason why clothing should be marketed to a specific gender only.

People should be free to enjoy expressing themselves through clothing without having to worry about what part of the store it came from and who the manufacturer is targeting.

There are many ways in which gender can be expressed—why limit this by sorting clothes in a particular way? CREATISTA/ISTOCK.COM

"Fashion should be about challenging the status quo."

—*Dilys Williams*

7

RAISING A
FASHION RUCKUS

MANY ASPECTS OF FASHION CAN BE ADJUSTED, built upon and used to change our world! Some people have taken these opportunities to the next level and started to change the world around them through fashion. From wearing clothing made from plastic water bottles on the red carpet to continuously crushing gender expectations to reducing body shaming, these people have created their own fashion ruckus. They have refused to accept the way things are and instead questioned how they can improve them.

JILLIAN OWENS

Jillian started her blog *ReFashionista* because she wanted to have new fashionable outfits but didn't want to buy unethically produced clothing. She decided that creating new outfits from cheap thrift-store finds would not only accomplish this but also help the environment. She uses a sewing machine, scissors and a measuring stick to create one-of-a-kind outfits that sometimes cost as little as a dollar! Jillian wanted to share her refashion designs through her blog so that even more people can become "refashionstas." She also shares her designs through social media, including her Instagram account, which has over 5,000 followers. You can even submit "reader refash" and be featured on the blog. Jillian's website says *ReFashion = Fashion Revisited, Repurposed, and Revitalized!*

JADEN SMITH

Jaden Smith is smashing gender stereotypes by just wearing what they want and showing others that you can be accepted (and celebrated) for doing the same. Jaden identifies as a non-binary gender, or "gender fluid," which means not exclusively male or female. Jaden also prefers to use *they* rather than *he* or *she*. Jaden chooses clothing that represents a form of self-expression for them, despite any pre-determined gender roles for those pieces of clothing. Jaden has designed many pieces that reflect their views on gender fluidity, and they were one of the faces for the Louis Vuitton Spring 2016 Womenswear Collection. Jaden has said their clothes are not "girls' clothes" or "boys' clothes" but just "clothes."

Jaden continues to question gender roles. They recently said, "Nobody ever thinks, 'Yo, who made all these rules? Who was here and made all these rules?' Because, I'm equally as smart as them, and I don't necessarily agree with all the rules that they established before I came into the picture."

You are definitely that smart too, so keep questioning the way things are and the way you want things to be!

JADEN IDENTIFIES AS
A NON-BINARY GENDER,
OR "GENDER FLUID,"
WHICH MEANS
NOT EXCLUSIVELY
MALE OR FEMALE.

Willow Smith and Jaden Smith pose on the red carpet while attending *Manus x Machina: Fashion in an Age of Technology* at the Metropolitan Museum of Art's Costume Institute Gala.

Before Gender-Specific Marketing

Clothing wasn't always so strictly gendered. President Franklin D. Roosevelt (1882–1945) can be seen wearing a dress (which we traditionally identify as being a woman's garment) in a baby picture. Boys and girls were dressed very similarly well into the twentieth century, when companies began marketing gender-specific clothing.

EMMA WATSON

In 2014, Emma Watson launched #HeForShe—
an international campaign for gender equality—
with UN Women (United Nations Entity for Gender
Equality and the Empowerment of Women). Even
before #HeForShe, Emma was a champion for a
more ethical world and for sustainable fashion. She
designed a fair-trade capsule collection in 2009 for
People Tree.

In 2016, Emma took her fashion consciousness to
the next level. At the 2016 Met Gala she wore an outfit
made out of recycled plastic bottles. It was designed
by Calvin Klein in collaboration with Eco-Age. Plastic
is one of the biggest pollutants on earth. Emma's
outfit consisted of an off-the-shoulder bustier,
wide-leg tailored pants and a long train. All parts were
detachable and intended to be reworn, so this piece
could have many uses and was not just designed to
be worn once, like many red-carpet dresses. Emma's
outfit made a strong statement: recycled clothing can
be fashionable *and* help our environment.

Emma Watson at the *Manus x Machina: Fashion in an Age of Technology* exhibition at the Metropolitan Museum of Art's Costume Institute Gala. Her dress made headlines due to its environmental statement.
NAOVIDIU HRUBARU/SHUTTERSTOCK.COM

The Green Carpet Challenge

Emma Watson's Met Gala dress was created as part of the Green Carpet Challenge, which encourages celebrities to promote more sustainable styles when they walk the red carpet. This challenge gives more exposure to the huge potential of ethical and sustainable fashion.

MELISSA MCCARTHY

In 2015, Melissa McCarthy launched her first fashion line. Its name is Seven7, and it's now available in major department stores across North America and online. Each item is available in sizes 4 to 28, and the goal of the collection is to create "comfortable clothes and accessories for women" and also "break down barriers in the fashion industry."

Melissa doesn't want her fashion line to be labeled "plus size," which has the effect of body-shaming customers. She has asked stores not to display her clothing in a separate section. And they've listened—all outlets that carry her line have changed their ways for Seven7.

In the United States, over 70 percent of women are "plus size" (over a size 14). Yet lots of larger retailers, such as Gap and H&M, only sell larger sizes online or in outlet malls, excluding those women from being able to shop in person at their main stores. Melissa McCarthy says this reinforces the destructive message that you're not really worthy unless your body is a certain size.

"As long as everybody's healthy, enjoy and embrace whatever body type you have."

—*Melissa McCarthy*

Melissa McCarthy poses at the *Ghostbusters* premiere in Los Angeles, 2016.

EREK HANSEN

When Erek Hansen was nine years old, he read about how recycled jeans can be made into insulation for new houses. He thought he could make a difference by collecting used jeans and donating them to the organization that makes Ultra-Touch Denim Insulation. This insulation is used to build houses for people whose homes have been destroyed by natural disasters.

Erek held a number of Denim Drives and collected mountains of used jeans. In 2015, Erek was sixteen and had done the project for seven years in a row! He also created Go Green Ohio, which supports other green clothing campaigns, such as collecting used shoes to be donated to those in need or turned into carpet padding, playground mulch, and athletic surfaces. You can hold your own Denim Drive to fundraise for BlueJeansGoGreen.org. Learn more about how Erek organizes his events on his website—www.GoGreenOhio.org.

In 2016, after ten years of the Blue Jeans Go Green denim-recycling program, the project was celebrated with a pop-up gallery in New York City. Here, founder Erek Hansen poses with actress Olivia Culpo. AMY HANSEN

STYLE TO STR
Step 02
Step 03
Once it's worn, you can continue its purpose by
of textiles thrown out every year.

THE MIND OF KYE

Kyemah McEntyre experienced bullying throughout high school, but when she graduated in 2015, she decided to respond to it in a creative way. Kyemah (MindofKye on Instagram) designed her own prom dress, which celebrated her African roots, individuality and creativity. Her original Instagram prom post said *Don't let anyone define you. Beautiful things happen when you take pride in yourself. #blackgirlsrock #kyebreaktheinternet.*

The original post has over 10,000 Likes, and media outlets picked up the story worldwide. Kye's dress went viral, and she is now studying fashion design at Parsons School of Design in New York City. She also designed a red-carpet dress for actor Naturi Naughton for the BET Awards 2015. That dress celebrated Naturi's heritage and culture. In 2016, Kye launched her first-ever collection and reminded the world to celebrate individuality and respond to hate with creativity and positivity.

Kyemah McEntyre arrives on the red carpet at the BET Honors Awards in 2016 in Washington, DC. JAMIE LAMOR THOMPSON/SHUTTERSTOCK.COM

"The more we stand up for it, the more we will see inclusion."
—*Verky Arcos Baldonado,*
editor-at-large, *Latina*

"Fast fashion isn't free. Someone, somewhere is paying."
—*Lucy Siegle*

"Do your little bit of good where you are; it's those little bits of good put together that overwhelm the world."
—*Archbishop Desmond Tutu*

"What a strange power there is in clothing."
—*Isaac Bashevis Singer*

8

BEYOND
YOUR OUTFIT

SO NOW YOU KNOW HOW TO FIND OUT where
your clothes come from, how to be a savvy shopper,
why you should question fashion messages and
what stories you'd like to tell the world through
your clothes. The best part of it all? You have a
choice each and every day to influence the world.
You can use this kind of decision making when
you buy anything—jewelry, accessories, hair products, makeup, a bike and much more. Choosing to
be conscious of your power goes beyond clothing.

It's a tool you can use to change the world in many more ways.

So always remember ...

SUPPORT POSITIVE PROJECTS

Sometimes it takes a bit of fashion detective work to find the right brands or products you want to support, but remember that every time you buy something, you have the opportunity to support and create positive change in the world.

CONTINUE TO QUESTION THINGS

It's important to continue to question the way things are and the way you want things to be. If you see something in the fashion world that you think could be improved, let it be known! Shine a light on an inequality you have discovered and make a plan for how you can change it. Show a company the way you want it to function through online campaigns, petitions, boycotts and other strategies. Continue to question and demand higher standards

#MyBodyMyBusiness

In London, Ontario, a female student named Laura Anderson was sent home from school in May 2015 to change because her outfit (ripped jeans and a tank top) was seen as a violation of her school's dress code. Many school dress codes almost exclusively penalize girls, usually for wearing clothing that is "not covering enough skin" or is "distracting." In response, Laura said, "My intention was not for it to be sexual... I have the right as an individual to wear what makes me feel comfortable." Other students agreed with Laura and protested by wearing tank tops and ripped jeans to school on the same day. They then uploaded pictures of these outfits under the hashtag #mybodymybusiness.

One student, Ashlyn Nicolle, also started a petition to support Laura. "In some situations where female students are asked to put sweaters on and 'cover up,' a message is implied that we as female students must cover up to ensure the male students are not distracted. These type of conditions in regards to female sexuality are sexist and outdated," she wrote on her Change.org page.

POP QUIZ

What do you think the world will look like in ten years?

Will the environment be healthier? Will we live in a more caring and accepting world? Will the world be free of child labor?

How do you want it to look?

How can you help to make that happen?

in our world. The moment you share an idea with the world, the closer it comes to reality.

START TODAY

The best thing about being part of this positive fashion revolution is that you can start today. Question the messages around you, continue to reduce, reuse and recycle in new ways, and start a conversation! It's all about making decisions to clothe yourself in a more globally conscious way.

"Be the change you want to see in the world."
—*Mahatma Gandhi*

"You cannot get through a single day without having an impact on the world around you. What you do makes a difference, and you have to decide what kind of difference you want to make."

—*Jane Goodall*

Dr. Jane Goodall is a primatologist, ethologist, anthropologist and UN Messenger of Peace. She is most famously known for her work with chimpanzees. Here she is seen interacting with local children in Taitung, Taiwan. CHIH CHANG CHOU/DREAMSTIME.COM

STAY CONNECTED

Continue the conversation and stay connected on PopActivism.com. *PopActivism* is a blog and online community I started in 2015. You can check it out online or submit your own contribution through the Contact section.

Throughout your new fashion detective work and activist adventures, you can stay connected to the PopActivist community through Twitter and Instagram @popactivism as well as by using the hashtag #popactivism.

Never simply accept the way things are. Instead, question how *you* can help improve them.

Remember: see change, share change, be change. And don't forget to send me a tweet @erinnep so I can retweet it!

SEE CHANGE, SHARE CHANGE, BE CHANGE.

Browsing through Fair Trade Certified clothing while trying on a sustainably sourced sweater. JENN PLAYFORD

GLOSSARY

biodegradable—capable of being broken down into harmless products by bacteria or other living organisms

bonded child labor, or debt slavery—the employment of children younger than eighteen, without their consent, to work off debts taken on by themselves or a family member/guardian

boycott—the act of refusing to use or buy products from, or deal with, a person, organization or country

charity—term used to describe an organization dedicated solely to helping others, not to making a profit or passing on profits to its members

child labor—the employment of children in any work that deprives them of their childhood, interferes with their ability to attend regular school and is mentally, physically, socially or morally dangerous and harmful

fair trade—a social movement that tries to help people in developing countries work in better conditions and get more money for what they make, without hurting the environment. A fair trade label on clothing indicates that the product was produced in a way that has a positive social, economic and environmental impact

fast fashion—an approach to the design, creation and marketing of clothing that focuses on making trendy clothing as cheaply and quickly as possible

for-profit—a term to describe an organization formed for the purpose of making money for itself/its members

global consciousness—the ability to see ourselves as part of a world community and understand the connections between our choices and the lives of others

global warming—the observed and anticipated increases in the average temperature of the earth's atmosphere and oceans

human rights—things we are allowed to be, to do or to have simply by being human, such as the right to food and a safe place to stay

influence—the power or capacity to bring about change

irrigate—to supply land or crops with water by artificial means such as pipes, sprinklers and canals

manifesto—a written statement that publicly declares your views, motives or intentions

nonprofit—term to describe an organization that focuses on activities that benefit society and uses profits to achieve its goals rather than to benefit its members or leaders

objectify—to treat someone as an object rather than a person

offshore—outside the country

organic—grown with fertilizers of plant or animal origin, such as manure, bone meal or compost, and without chemical fertilizers or pesticides

pesticide—a chemical or biological agent that discourages, weakens or kills pests

profit—the surplus remaining after a business's total costs are deducted from its total revenue

recycle—the process of converting waste materials into new materials and objects.

supply chain—the network of people and organizations involved in getting a product or service from suppliers to customers

sweatshop—a factory or workshop, especially in the clothing industry, that employs workers, sometimes children, for very low wages and long hours, often in poor working conditions

popactivism

see change. share change. be change.

RESOURCES

CHAPTER 1
www.malala.org

CHAPTER 2
www.otesha.ca/files/the_otesha_book.pdf
www.un.org/en/universal-declaration-human-rights
www.we.org

CHAPTER 3
www.change.org
www.fairtrade.ca
www.greenpeace.org
www.wto.org

CHAPTER 4
www.ecofashion-week.com
www.ecofashionworld.com
www.ecohabitude.com
www.enrou.com
www.thegoodtrade.com
www.stylewise-blog.com

CHAPTER 5
www.ethicalwriters.co
www.nastygal.com
www.poshmark.com
www.thesorrygirls.com
www.upcyclethat.com
www.yerdle.com

CHAPTER 6
http://truecostmovie.com

CHAPTER 7
www.eco-age.com/gcc-brandmark-brands
www.gogreenohio.org
www.refashionista.net

ACKNOWLEDGMENTS

FIRST AND FOREMOST, I WOULD LIKE TO ACKNOWLEDGE every person who has committed their life to fighting for the betterment of others. There are so many people who have inspired me throughout my life so far, from Malala Yousafzai to Elizabeth May to Alana Charlton to Sara Reside and many more.

Thank you once again to everyone who has supported this book and the mission it creates. To Trinity College at the University of Toronto, thank you for inspiring me and everyone else to do better. To my mother, father, and brother, Stuart, thank you for always being there. To Julia Tops, Allie Pritchard, Alex Pavel, Preet Walia, Sarah Kwajafa, Gabbi Leon, Rebecca Tran, Emily Faris and many others—thank you for showing the world what is possible when you work constantly from a place of determination and passion.

Thank you to Orca Book Publishers for believing in this project and helping it become a reality. To Sarah Harvey, thank you for not only helping to grow these books into what they are today but also supporting me in becoming a better author and creator. To Jenn Playford, thank you for believing in the vision of this book series and for shaping this book in particular into something I could never have imagined.

Finally, thank you to the St. Clair Balfour family and University of Toronto National Scholarship Program for giving me both the opportunity to attend U of T and the financial freedom to focus on these books throughout my undergraduate program.

ERINNE PAISLEY is an activist, public speaker, writer and student who made international headlines when she turned her math homework into a dress and wore it to her prom, then donated the money she would have spent on a dress to the Malala Fund. Now she is studying Peace, Conflict and Justice, as well as Book and Media Studies, at the University of Toronto. Erinne recently completed an internship at She's the First, an organization that provides scholarships, mentorship and empowerment to girls in low-income countries. She is the founder of PopActivism, a website devoted to promoting positive activism in pop culture.

Can Your Outfit Change the World? is her second book. For more information visit www.popactivism.com, or follow Erinne on social media.

    🐦 @ErinneP

    📷 @pop_activism

    ▶️ Erinne Paisley

LOOK FOR THE OTHER
TWO BOOKS IN THE

POPACTIVISM

2018

a
popactivism
book

nne
sley

ONS
RLD?

$14.95